How to do Accounting II

Table of Contents

STUDENT WORKING PAPERS

by James Foote

©2005 TX6- 255-315

Chapter	Problem	Page #
Chapter 10	Employee Payroll Taxes	3 - 9
	Payroll Register 10.1 10.2 & 10.3	3
	Mecon's 'Magic Gail's Goods	4
	Mike Brandon 10.2	5
	Brandon's Ledger 10.2	5 - 9
Chapter 11	Employer's Payroll Taxes	11 - 15
	Brandon's Payroll Register 11.2	11 & 12
	Brandon's Cash Journal 11.2	13 & 14
	Brandon's Trial Balance 11.2	15
Chapter 12	Purchases and Sales Discounts	16 - 31
	Edwards Purchases & Tipton"s Sales 12.2 & 12.3	16
	Edwards Cash Journal	17
	Tipton's Cash Journal	18
	Hart & Son Cash Journal 12.4 & 13.4	19 & 20
	Hart & Son Trial Balance 12.4	21
	Hart & Son Purchases and Sales Journals 12.4	22
	Hart & Son General Ledger 12.4, 13.4, 15.4	23 – 29
	Hart & Son Accounts Receivable Ledger 12.4	30
	Hart & Son Accounts Payable Ledger 12.4	31
Chapter 13	Purchases and Sales Adjustments	32 -35
	Reynold's Inc Cash Journal 13.2	32
	Roller Cash Journal 13.3	33
	Hart & Son Trial Balance 13.4	34 & 35

How to do Accounting II
STUDENT WORKING PAPERS

Chapter	Problem	Page #
Chapter 14	Current Assets	36 - 39
	Tittle and Molly's Motors General Journal 14.1 & 14.3	36
	Q. D. Shanks Lumber Calculations 14.2	37
	Hart & Son Worksheet 14.4	38 - 39
Chapter 15	Depreciation of Fixed Assets	40 - 43
	Calculations 15.2 & 15.3 & Sparks Brothers Gen Journal	40
	Mary Foxx Cash Journal 15.3	41
	Hart & Son Income, Capital and Balance Sheet	42 & 43
Chapter 16	Accrual Accounting	44 - 57
	Calculations and General Journal for 16.1	44
	Lane's Calculations and General Journal 16.2	45
	Molly Eloise Work Sheet 16.3	46 & 47
	Hart & Son General Journal Adjusting, Closing 16.4	48 & 49
	Hart & Son General Ledger 16.4	50 – 56
	Hart & Son Post Closing Trial Balance 16.4	57
Chapter 17	Sales Tax and Credit card Sales	58 – 61
	Meg's Muffler Calculations and General Journal 17.1	58
	Marquit's Boutique Cash Journal 17.2	59
	Molly Eloise Income, Capital and Balance Sheet 17.3	60 & 61
Chapter 18	Capital Section	62 – 65
	Mallett & Foote General Journal & Capital Statement 18.1	62
	We Care Lawn Care General Journal 18.2	63
	Molly Eloise General Journal Adjusting, Closing 18.3	64 & 65

Maeve's Magic Make-over

PAYROLL REGISTER

Date

NAME	EARNINGS			DEDUCTIONS						Net Pay
10.1	Regular	Overtime	Total Pay	Fed Income Tx	Soc. Sec. Tax	Medicare Tax	401-K	United Way		Net Pay
Jacob Job										
Mel Malone										
Sandra S.										
Sally Smith										
Jennifer B.										

GAIL'S GOODS Payroll Register

NAME	EARNINGS			DEDUCTIONS						Net Pay
10.3	Regular	Overtime	Total Pay	Fed Income Tx	Soc. Sec. Tax	Medicare Tax	State & Local	United Way		Net Pay
Jim Metro										
Helen Lake										
Joe Salt										
Peg Pepper										
Chris Jack										

BRANDON'S PAYROLL REGISTER

NAME	EARNINGS			DEDUCTIONS						Net Pay
10.2	Regular	Overtime	Total Pay	Fed Income Tx	Soc. Sec. Tax	Medicare Tax	Child Care	United Way		Net Pay
Shirley J										
Liam Foote										
Dick Reed										
Karen M										
Tom Jones										

10.1 Maeve's Magic Make-over
GENERAL JOURNAL
Page_____

	DATE		DESCRIPTION	PR	DEBIT	CREDIT
1						
2						
3						
4						
5						
6						
7						
8						
9						
10						
11						
12						

10.3 Gail's Goods
GENERAL JOURNAL
Page_____

1						
2						
3						
4						
5						
6						
7						
8						
9						
10						
11						
12						
13						
14						
15						
16						

BRANDON'S

Problem # 10.2   **CASH JOURNAL**   Page_____

CASH		DATE		DESCRIPTION	Post	GENERAL	
Debit	Credit	Month	Day		Ref	Debit	Credit

Problem #10.2 & 11.2   **BRANDON'S**
GENERAL LEDGER

Account   **CASH**   No. 110

DATE	ITEM	PR	Debit	Credit	BALANCE Debit	BALANCE Credit

Account   **CASH - PAYROLL**   No. 115

DATE	ITEM	PR	Debit	Credit	BALANCE Debit	BALANCE Credit

Account   **OFFICE SUPPLIES**   No. 120

DATE	ITEM	PR	Debit	Credit	BALANCE Debit	BALANCE Credit

Account   **INVENTORY**   No. 125

DATE	ITEM	PR	Debit	Credit	BALANCE Debit	BALANCE Credit

10.2 Brandon's General Ledger page 2

Account **ACCOUNTS PAYABLE**   No. 210

DATE	ITEM	PR	Debit	Credit	BALANCE Debit	BALANCE Credit

Account **FEDERAL INCOME TAX PAYABLE**   No. 220

DATE	ITEM	PR	Debit	Credit	BALANCE Debit	BALANCE Credit

Account **FICA PAYABLE**   No. 222

DATE	ITEM	PR	Debit	Credit	BALANCE Debit	BALANCE Credit

Account **MEDICARE PAYABLE**   No. 225

DATE	ITEM	PR	Debit	Credit	BALANCE Debit	BALANCE Credit

Account **CHILD CARE PAYABLE**   No. 230

DATE	ITEM	PR	Debit	Credit	BALANCE Debit	BALANCE Credit

Account **UNITED WAY PAYABLE**   No. 232

DATE	ITEM	PR	Debit	Credit	BALANCE Debit	BALANCE Credit

Account **FEDERAL UNEMPLOYMENT PAYABLE**   No. 240

DATE	ITEM	PR	Debit	Credit	BALANCE Debit	BALANCE Credit

Account **STATE UNEMPLOYMENT PAYABLE**   No. 242

DATE	ITEM	PR	Debit	Credit	BALANCE Debit	BALANCE Credit

Account **NOTES PAYABLE**   No. 250

DATE	ITEM	PR	Debit	Credit	BALANCE Debit	BALANCE Credit

Account **MIKE BRANDON, CAPITAL**   No. 310

DATE	ITEM	PR	Debit	Credit	BALANCE	
					Debit	Credit

Account **MIKE BRANDON, DRAWING**   No. 320

DATE	ITEM	PR	Debit	Credit	BALANCE	
					Debit	Credit

Account **SALES**   No. 410

DATE	ITEM	PR	Debit	Credit	BALANCE	
					Debit	Credit

Account **PURCHASES**   No. 510

DATE	ITEM	PR	Debit	Credit	BALANCE	
					Debit	Credit

Account **ADVERTISING EXPENSE**   No. 520

DATE	ITEM	PR	Debit	Credit	BALANCE	
					Debit	Credit

Account **EMPLOYER PAYROLL TAX EXPENSE**   No. 530

DATE	ITEM	PR	Debit	Credit	BALANCE Debit	Credit

Account **RENT EXPENSE**   No. 535

DATE	ITEM	PR	Debit	Credit	BALANCE Debit	Credit

Account **UTILITIES EXPENSE**   No. 540

DATE	ITEM	PR	Debit	Credit	BALANCE Debit	Credit

Account **WAGE & SALARY EXPENSE**   No. 550

DATE	ITEM	PR	Debit	Credit	BALANCE Debit	Credit

Account   No.

DATE	ITEM	PR	Debit	Credit	BALANCE Debit	Credit

11. 2 Brandon's Payroll Register

BRANDON'S PAYROLL REGISTER
Date May 30, 20

NAME	EARNINGS			DEDUCTIONS					Net Pay
11.2	Regular	Overtime	Total Pay	Fed Income Tx	Soc. Sec. Tax	Medicare Tax	Child Care	United Way	
Shirley J									
Liam Foote									
Dick Reed									
Karen M									
Tom Jones									

BRANDON'S PAYROLL REGISTER
Date June 15, 20

NAME	EARNINGS			DEDUCTIONS					Net Pay
11.2	Regular	Overtime	Total Pay	Fed Income Tx	Soc. Sec. Tax	Medicare Tax	Child Care	United Way	
Shirley J									
Liam Foote									
Dick Reed									
Karen M									
Tom Jones									

BRANDON'S PAYROLL REGISTER
Date June 30, 20

NAME	EARNINGS			DEDUCTIONS					Net Pay
11.2	Regular	Overtime	Total Pay	Fed Income Tx	Soc. Sec. Tax	Medicare Tax	Child Care	United Way	
Shirley J									
Liam Foote									
Dick Reed									
Karen M									
Tom Jones									

11.2 Brandon's Taxable Earnings Table

BRANDON'S Taxable Earnings Table
Date May 15, 20

NAME	EARNINGS		DEDUCTIONS				
11.2	Accumulated	Pay Period	Taxable	Amout Taxed	FUTA	SUTA	FICA	Medicar	Other
Shirley J									
Liam Foote									
Dick Reed									
Karen M									
Tom Jones									

BRANDON'S Taxable Earnings Table
Date May 30, 20

NAME	EARNINGS		DEDUCTIONS				
11.2	Accumulated	Pay Period	Taxable	Amout Taxed	FUTA	SUTA	FICA	Medicar	Other
Shirley J									
Liam Foote									
Dick Reed									
Karen M									
Tom Jones									

BRANDON'S Taxable Earnings Table
Date June 15, 20

NAME	EARNINGS		DEDUCTIONS				
11.2	Accumulated	Pay Period	Taxable	Amout Taxed	FUTA	SUTA	FICA	Medicar	Other
Shirley J									
Liam Foote									
Dick Reed									
Karen M									
Tom Jones									

BRANDON'S Taxable Earnings Table
Date June 30, 20

NAME	EARNINGS		DEDUCTIONS				
11.2	Accumulated	Pay Period	Taxable	Amout Taxed	FUTA	SUTA	FICA	Medicar	Other
Shirley J									
Liam Foote									
Dick Reed									
Karen M									
Tom Jones									

11.2

Brandon

CASH JOURNAL

Student Name_____

Page_____

CASH		DATE		DESCRIPTION	Post	GENERAL	
Debit	Credit	Month	Day		Ref	Debit	Credit

11.2

Brandon

Student Name_____

CASH JOURNAL

Page_____

| CASH | | DATE | | DESCRIPTION | Post | GENERAL | |
Debit	Credit	Month	Day		Ref	Debit	Credit

11.2				Student Name_____	

Brandon's

Trial Balance

Page_____

	ACCOUNT NAME	PR	DEBIT	CREDIT
1				
2				
3				
4				
5				
6				
7				
8				
9				
10				
11				
12				
13				
14				
15				
16				
17				
18				
19				
20				
21				
22				
23				
24				
25				
26				
27				
28				
29				
30				
31				

Students Name_____

Mark Edwards Company
12.2 **PURCHASES JOURNAL** Page_____

	DATE	Dis	Name of Account	Post Ref	Purchases Debit Accounts Pay. Cr.				
1									
2									
3									
4									
5									
6									
7									
8									
9									
10									
11									
12									
13									
14									

Tipton's Toy World
12.3 **SALES JOURNAL** Page_____

	DATE	Dis	Name of Account	Post Ref	Accounts Rec. Debit Sales Credit				
1									
2									
3									
4									
5									
6									
7									
8									
9									
10									
11									
12									

CASH		DATE		DESCRIPTION	Post	GENERAL	
Debit	Credit	Month	Day		Ref	Debit	Credit
64,367.00	36,181.05					63,697.71	91,883.66

Edwards Company

CASH JOURNAL

12.2

Student Name_____

Page_____

Tipton"s Toy World

CASH JOURNAL

12.3

Student Name_____

Page_____

| CASH | | DATE | | DESCRIPTION | Post | GENERAL | |
Debit	Credit	Month	Day		Ref	Debit	Credit

Hart & Son
CASH JOURNAL

12.4 &13.4

Student Name_____

Page_____

CASH		DATE		DESCRIPTION	Post	GENERAL	
Debit	Credit	Month	Day		Ref	Debit	Credit
13,168.22	29,072.60					55,956.68	40,052.30

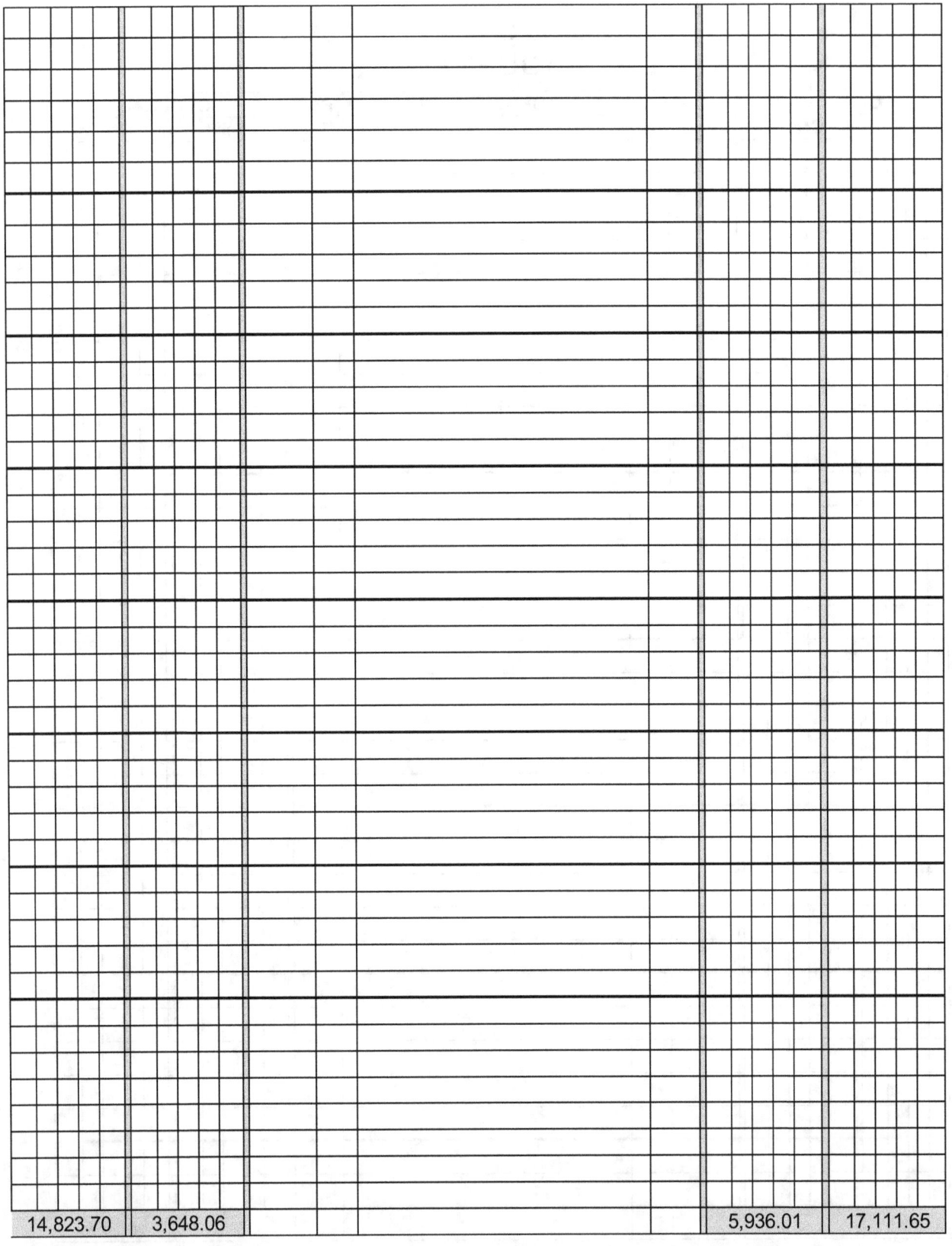

14,823.70	3,648.06					5,936.01	17,111.65

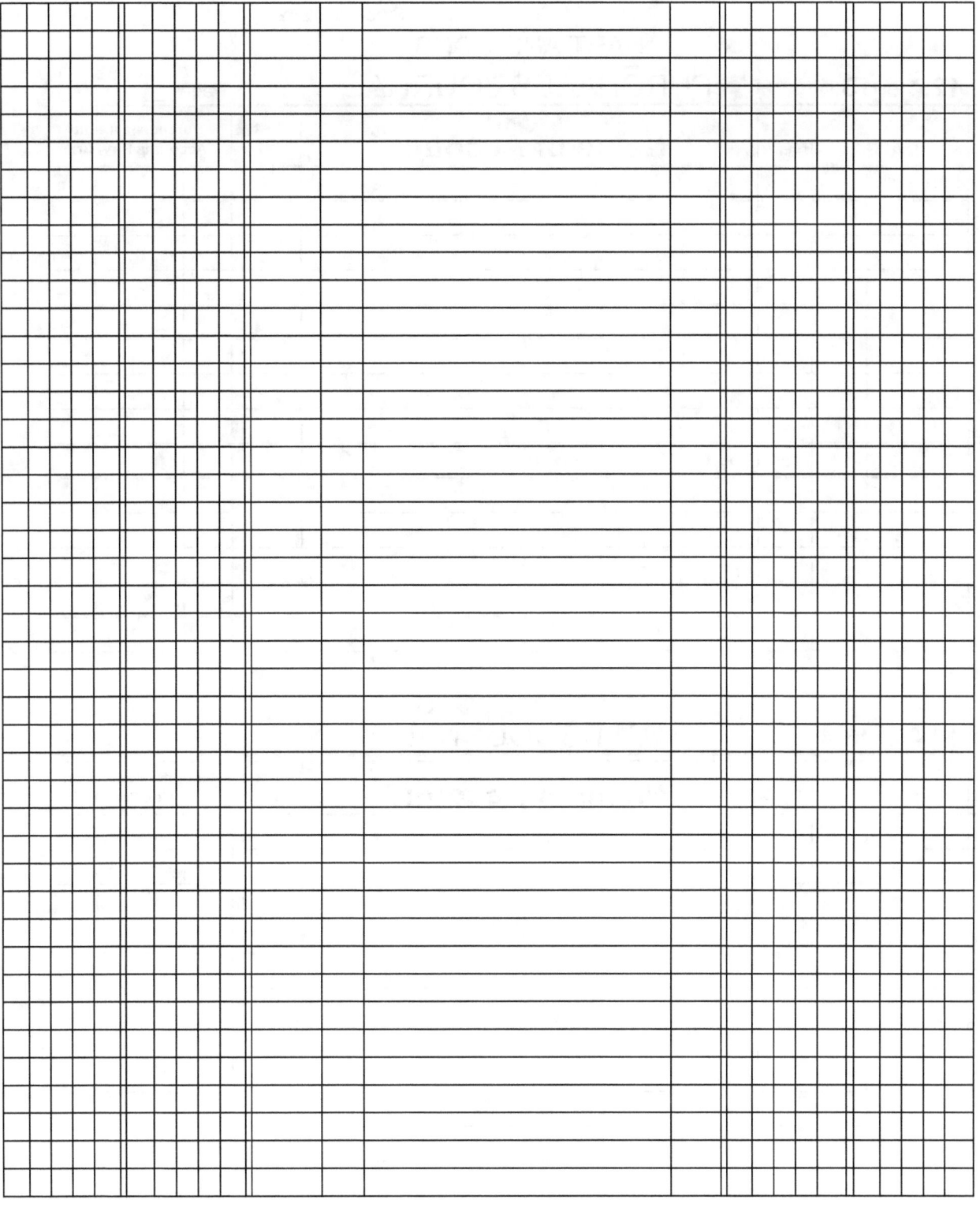

12.4 13.4 Hart and Son Purchases and Sales Journal

Students Name_____

HART AND SONS

12.4 & 13.4 **PURCHASES JOURNAL** Page_____

	DATE		Dis	Name of Account	Post Ref		Purchases Debit Accounts Pay. Cr.				
1											
2											
3											
4											
5											
6											
7											
8											
9											
10											
11											
12											
13											
14											

HART AND SONS

12.4 & 13.4 **SALES JOURNAL** Page_____

	DATE		Dis	Name of Account	Post Ref		Accounts Rec. Debit Sales Credit				
1											
2											
3											
4											
5											
6											
7											
8											
9											
10											
11											
12											

Student Name_____

12.4 & 13.4

HART & SON
GENERAL LEDGER

Account **CASH**   No. 110

DATE		ITEM	PR	Debit	Credit	BALANCE Debit	BALANCE Credit
Oct	31	Balance				$26,568.14	

Account **CASH - PAYROLL**   No. 115

DATE	ITEM	PR	Debit	Credit	BALANCE Debit	BALANCE Credit

Account **ACCOUNTS RECEIVABLE**   No. 120

DATE	ITEM	PR	Debit	Credit	BALANCE Debit	BALANCE Credit

Account **ALLOWANCE FOR DOUBTFUL ACCOUNTS**   No. 125

DATE		ITEM	PR	Debit	Credit	BALANCE Debit	BALANCE Credit
Oct	31	Balance					$139.24

Account **OFFICE SUPPLIES**   No. 130

DATE		ITEM	PR	Debit	Credit	BALANCE Debit	BALANCE Credit
Oct	31	Balance				$321.82	

Account **OFFICE EQUIPMENT**   No. 140

DATE		ITEM	PR	Debit	Credit	BALANCE Debit	BALANCE Credit
Oct	31	Balance				$10,863.21	

Account **ALLOWANCE DEPRECIATION OFFICE EQUIPMENT**   No. 140

DATE		ITEM	PR	Debit	Credit	BALANCE Debit	BALANCE Credit
Oct	31	Balance					$2,683.21

Account **DELIVERY TRUCK**   No. 150

DATE		ITEM	PR	Debit	Credit	BALANCE Debit	BALANCE Credit

Account **ALLOWANCE FOR DEPRECIATION TRUCK**   No. 155

DATE		ITEM	PR	Debit	Credit	BALANCE Debit	BALANCE Credit

Account **INVENTORY**   No. 160

DATE		ITEM	PR	Debit	Credit	BALANCE Debit	BALANCE Credit
Oct	31	Balance				$8,000.00	

Account FEDERAL INCOME TAX PAYABLE · No. 205

| | | | | | BALANCE | |
DATE	ITEM	PR	Debit	Credit	Debit	Credit

Account FICA PAYABLE · No. 207

| | | | | | BALANCE | |
DATE	ITEM	PR	Debit	Credit	Debit	Credit

Account MEDICARE PAYABLE · No. 208

| | | | | | BALANCE | |
DATE	ITEM	PR	Debit	Credit	Debit	Credit

Account ACCOUNTS PAYABLE · No. 210

| | | | | | BALANCE | |
DATE	ITEM	PR	Debit	Credit	Debit	Credit
Oct 31	Balance					$1,000.00

Account FUTA PAYABLE · No. 220

| | | | | | BALANCE | |
DATE	ITEM	PR	Debit	Credit	Debit	Credit

Account **STATE EMPLOYMENT PAYABLE**   No. 222

DATE	ITEM	PR	Debit	Credit	BALANCE	
					Debit	Credit

Account **INTEREST PAYABLE**   No. 225

DATE	ITEM	PR	Debit	Credit	BALANCE	
					Debit	Credit

Account **WAGES PAYABLE**   No. 230

DATE	ITEM	PR	Debit	Credit	BALANCE	
					Debit	Credit

Account **NOTES PAYABLE**   No. 240

DATE	ITEM	PR	Debit	Credit	BALANCE	
					Debit	Credit

Account **HART & SONS, CAPITAL**   No. 310

DATE	ITEM	PR	Debit	Credit	BALANCE	
					Debit	Credit
Oct 31	Balance					$41,930.72

Account **HART & SONS, DRAWING**   No. 315

DATE	ITEM	PR	Debit	Credit	BALANCE	
					Debit	Credit

Account **INCOME SUMMARY**   No. 330

DATE	ITEM	PR	Debit	Credit	BALANCE Debit	Credit

Account **SALES**   No. 410

DATE	ITEM	PR	Debit	Credit	BALANCE Debit	Credit

Account **SALES DISCOUNT**   No. 415

DATE	ITEM	PR	Debit	Credit	BALANCE Debit	Credit

Account **SALES RETURNS AND ALLOWANCES**   No. 420

DATE	ITEM	PR	Debit	Credit	BALANCE Debit	Credit

Account **PURCHASES**   No. 510

DATE	ITEM	PR	Debit	Credit	BALANCE Debit	Credit

Account **PURCHASES DISCOUNT**   No. 515

DATE	ITEM	PR	Debit	Credit	BALANCE Debit	BALANCE Credit

Account **PURCHASES RETURNS AND ALLOWANCES**   No. 520

DATE	ITEM	PR	Debit	Credit	BALANCE Debit	BALANCE Credit

Account **RENT EXPENSE**   No. 525

DATE	ITEM	PR	Debit	Credit	BALANCE Debit	BALANCE Credit

Account **EMPLOYER PAYROLL EXPENSES**   No. 530

DATE	ITEM	PR	Debit	Credit	BALANCE Debit	BALANCE Credit

Account **DOUBTFUL ACCOUNTS EXPENSE**   No. 535

DATE	ITEM	PR	Debit	Credit	BALANCE Debit	BALANCE Credit

Account **UTILITIES EXPENSE**   No. 540

DATE	ITEM	PR	Debit	Credit	BALANCE Debit	BALANCE Credit

Account **WAGE EXPENSE**   No. 545

DATE	ITEM	PR	Debit	Credit	BALANCE Debit	BALANCE Credit

Account **DEPRECIATION EXPENSE**   No. 555

DATE	ITEM	PR	Debit	Credit	BALANCE Debit	BALANCE Credit

Account **OFFICE SUPPLIES EXPENSE**   No. 560

DATE	ITEM	PR	Debit	Credit	BALANCE Debit	BALANCE Credit

Account **INTEREST EXPENSE**   No. 565

DATE	ITEM	PR	Debit	Credit	BALANCE Debit	BALANCE Credit

Account **MISCELLANEOUS EXPENSE**   No. 575

DATE	ITEM	PR	Debit	Credit	BALANCE Debit	BALANCE Credit

Student Name_____

Hart & Sons
ACCOUNTS RECEIVABLE LEDGER

HILL AND DAUGHTER   Account # 71

DATE		ITEM	Post			DEBIT
Month	Day		Ref	Debit	Credit	Balance

WOODS WORLD   Account # 72

DATE		ITEM	Post			DEBIT
Month	Day		Ref	Debit	Credit	Balance

Schedule of Accounts Receivable and Payable for Hart & Sons

Account #	Name	Amount

Account #	Name	Amount

Student Name_____

HART & SONS

ACCOUNTS PAYABLE LEDGER

Problem 12.4 & 13.4

Company Name **ACE SUPPLY**   Account # #

DATE		ITEM	Post					CREDIT
Month	Day		Ref	Debit		Credit		Balance

Company Name **LEWIS BROTHERS**   Account # #

DATE		ITEM	Post					CREDIT
Month	Day		Ref	Debit		Credit		Balance

Company Name **LYLE & SONS**   Account # #

DATE		ITEM	Post					CREDIT
Month	Day		Ref	Debit		Credit		Balance

Company Name **TWIN SISTERS**   Account # #

DATE		ITEM	Post					CREDIT
Month	Day		Ref	Debit		Credit		Balance

Reynold's Inc

Student Name_____

13.2 CASH JOURNAL

Page_____

CASH		DATE		DESCRIPTION	Post	GENERAL	
Debit	Credit	Month	Day		Ref	Debit	Credit
15,891.50	1,939.75					19,277.85	33,229.60

Roller & Son

Problem # 13.3

CASH JOURNAL

Student Name_____

Page_____

| CASH | | DATE | | DESCRIPTION | Post | GENERAL | |
Debit	Credit	Month	Day		Ref	Debit	Credit
0.00	20,478.54					68,315.66	47,837.12

Student Name_____

HART & SON
Trial Balance

13.4   Page_____

	ACCOUNT NAME	PR	DEBIT	CREDIT
1				
2				
3				
4				
5				
6				
7				
8				
9				
10				
11				
12				
13				
14				
15				
16				
17				
18				
19				
20				
21				
22				
23				
24				
25				
26				
27				
28				
29				
30				
31				

Student Name_____

HART & SON
Trial Balance

13.4

Page_____

		ACCOUNT NAME	PR	DEBIT	CREDIT
1					
2					
3					
4					
5					
6					
7					
8					
9					
10					
11					
12					
13					
14					
15					
16					
17					
18					
19					
20					
21					
22					
23					
24					
25					
26					
27					
28					
29					
30					
31	Worksheet 14.4 for account balances to total			$110,144.11	$110,144.11

14.1 Tittle Tile General Journal
14.2 Molly's Motors General Journal

Student Name_____

Tittle Tile
14.1 GENERAL JOURNAL

Page_____

	DATE		DESCRIPTION	PR	DEBIT	CREDIT
1						
2						
3						
4						
5						
6						
7						
8						
9						
10						
11						
12						
13						
14						
15						
16						

Molly's Motors
14.3 GENERAL JOURNAL

Page_____

	DATE		DESCRIPTION	PR	DEBIT	CREDIT
1						
2						
3						
4						
5						
6						
7						
8						
9						
10						
11						
12						
13						

14.2 Q. D. Shanks Lumber Yard

Students Name_____

Q. D. Shanks Lumber Yard
Inventory Adjustments

Problem 14.2

#1	Average	LIFO	FIFO
Hammer	$55.23	$86.70	$43.00

	Number	Price	Total
Beginning	15	8.67	130.05
Purchase #1	25	5.83	145.75
Purchase #2	50	4.50	225.00
Purchase #3	20	5.95	119.00
Purchase #4	10	4.30	43.00
Total	120		
Ending Inv.	10		662.80

#2	Average	LIFO	FIFO
Sander			$1,965.00

	Number	Price	Total
Beginning	5	350.00	
Purchase #1	2	375.00	
Purchase #2	1	425.00	
Purchase #3	2	375.00	
Purchase #4	2	395.00	
Ending Inv.	5		

#3	Average	LIFO	FIFO
18' Pine	$13,539.71		

	Number	Price	Total
Beginning	400	16.00	
Purchase #1	500	15.00	
Purchase #2	1,000	14.25	
Purchase #3	1,000	14.00	
Purchase #4	500	18.00	
Ending Inv.	900		

#4	Average	LIFO	FIFO
4x8 Sheets		$1,110.00	

	Number	Price	Total
Beginning			
Purchase #1			
Purchase #2			
Purchase #3			
Purchase #4			
Ending Inv.			

#5	Average	LIFO	FIFO
3" Nails			

	Number	Price	Total
Beginning			
Purchase #1			
Purchase #2			
Purchase #3			
Purchase #4			
Ending Inv.			

#	Average	LIFO	FIFO

	Number	Price	Total
Beginning			
Purchase #1			
Purchase #2			
Purchase #3			
Purchase #4			
Ending Inv.			

14.4

Company **HART & SONS**

Worksheet

Date _____ Student Name _____

ACCOUNT	TRIAL BALANCE Debit	TRIAL BALANCE Credit	ADJUSTMENTS COLUMN Debit	ADJUSTMENTS COLUMN Credit	E - INCOME STATEMENT - I Debit	E - INCOME STATEMENT - I Credit	A - BALANCE SHEET - L & C Debit	A - BALANCE SHEET - L & C Credit
1 Cash	21,839.40							
2 Accounts Receivable	8,797.68							
3 Allow Doubt Accounts		139.24						
4 Office Supplies	710.82							
5 Office Equipment	13,541.21							
6 Allow. for Dep. Off Eq		2,683.21						
7 Delivery Truck	27,000.00							
8 Allow for Dep Del Eq								
9 Inventory	8,000.00							
10 Fed Income Tax Pay		98.50						
11 FICA Payable		229.66						
12 Medicare Pay		24.36						
13 Accounts Payable		6,113.80						
14 FUTA Payable		107.44						
15 State Emp Payable		67.15						
16 Interest Payable								
17 Wages Payable								
18 Notes Payable		19,500.00						
19 Hart & Sons, Capital		41,930.72						
20 Hart & Sons, Drawing	500.00							

14.4 Hart and Sons Worksheet page 2

#	Account	Debit	Credit
1	Income Summary		
2	Sales		38,209.59
3	Sales Discount	480.99	
4	Sales Returns & Allow.	939.00	
5	Purchases	23,736.60	
6	Purchases Discount		347.44
7	Purchases Ret. & Allow		693.00
8	Rent Expense	2,400.00	
9	Employer Payroll Ex	301.60	
10	Bad Debts Expense		
11	Utilities Expense	520.00	
12	Wage Expense	1,343.00	
13	Depreciation Expense		
14	Office Supplies Expens	28.98	
15	Interest Expense		
16	Miscellaneous Expense	4.83	
17		110,144.11	110,144.11
18			
19			
20			
22			

Totals columns:

		$21,749.30
		$21,749.30
34,904.30	4,945.73	$39,850.03
39,850.03		$39,850.03
80,607.29		$80,607.29
75,661.56	4,945.73	$80,607.29

Student Name_____

Sparks Brothers
15.2 GENERAL JOURNAL Page_____

	DATE		DESCRIPTION	PR	DEBIT	CREDIT
1						
2						
3						
4						
5						
6						
7						
8						
9						
10						
11						
12						
13						
14						
15						
16						

1						
2						
3						
4						
5						
6						
7						
8						
9						
10						
11						
12						
13						

Student Name_____

Mary Foxx
CASH JOURNAL

15.3

Page_____

CASH		DATE		DESCRIPTION	Post	GENERAL	
Debit	Credit	Month	Day		Ref	Debit	Credit

Student Name_____

HART & SONS
Income Statement

15.4

	Accounts																	
1																		
2																		
3																		
4																		
5																		
6																		
7																		
8																		
9																		
10																		
11																		
12																		
13																		
14																		
15																		
16																		
17																		
18																		
19																		
20																		
21																		
22																		
23																		
24																		
25																		
26																		

HART & SONS
Capital Statement

15.4

1									
2									
3									
4									
5									
6									

HART & SONS
Balance Sheet

	Accounts								
1									
2									
3									
4									
5									
6									
7									
8									
9									
10									
11									
12									
13									
14									
15									
16									
17									
18									
19									
20									
21									
22									
23									

16.1 Sparks Brothers

Student Name_____

Sparks Brothers
16.1   GENERAL JOURNAL   Page_____

	DATE		DESCRIPTION	PR	DEBIT	CREDIT
1						
2						
3						
4						
5						
6						
7						
8						
9						
10						
11						
12						
13						
14						
15						
16						

1						
2						
3						
4						
5						
6						
7						
8						
9						
10						
11						
12						
13						

Student Name_____

LANE'S Luxury Limousine Service
16.2   # GENERAL JOURNAL

Page_____

	DATE		DESCRIPTION	PR	DEBIT	CREDIT
1						
2						
3						
4						
5						
6						
7						
8						
9						
10						
11						
12						
13						
14						
15						
16						
17						
18						
19						
20						
21						
22						
23						
24						
25						
26						
27						
28						
29						
30						

16.3

MOLLY ELOISE MATERIALS

Company _____

Worksheet

Date _____

Student Name _____

ACCOUNT	TRIAL BALANCE Debit	TRIAL BALANCE Credit	ADJUSTMENTS COLUMN Debit	ADJUSTMENTS COLUMN Credit	E - INCOME STATEMENT - I Debit	E - INCOME STATEMENT - I Credit	A - BALANCE SHEET - L & C Debit	A - BALANCE SHEET - L & C Credit
1 Cash	33,673.21							
2 Accounts Receivable	35,385.13							
3 Allow Doubt Accounts		28.50						
4 Office Supplies	1,863.48							
5 Store Selling Supplies	1,258.65							
6 Shipping Supplies	183.22							
7 Postage	110.00							
8 Pre Paid Insur. Office	2,421.55							
9 Pre Paid Insur. Truck	1,843.00							
10 Office Equipment	25,681.29							
11 Allow. for Dep. Off Eq		10,338.25						
12 Delivery Truck	40,365.00							
13 Allow for Dep Del Eq		14,200.00						
14 Inventory	15,698.56							
15 Fed Income Tax Pay		3,851.87						
16 FICA Payable		1,764.10						
17 Medicare Pay		185.43						
18 Accounts Payable		8,879.62						
19 FUTA Payable		2,461.76						
20 State Emp Payable		1,527.91						
21 Interest Payable								
22 Wages Payable								
23 Notes Payable		25,831.60						
24 Molly E Foote, Capital		31,069.39						
25 Molly E. Foote, Drawing	3,385.00							

16.3 Molly Eloise Materials Page 2

#	Account							
26	Income Summary							
27	Sales	153,735.06						
28	Sales Discount	2,538.16						
29	Sales Returns & Allow.	4,147.75						
30	Purchases	46,315.43						
31	Purchases Discount		2,189.51					
32	Purchases Ret. & Allow		3,392.08					
33	Rent Expense	8,600.00						
34	Employer Payroll Ex	2,384.54						
35	Bad Debts Expense							
36	Utilities Expense	3,426.95						
37	Wage Expense	30,146.53						
38	Depreciation Expense							
39	Office Supplies Expense							
40	Store Sell Supp Expense							
41	Ship Sup & Postage Ex							
42	Insurance Expense							
43	Interest Expense							
44	Miscellaneous Expense	27.63						
		259,455.08	259,455.08					
		0.00						

Column totals (across pages): $46,146.82 $119,477.19 $159,316.65 $154,290.61 $114,451.15

Adjustments:

Allow for Bad Debts	2% of AR	Inventory	$12,128.31
Office Supplies on Han	953.92		
Store Sell Supp on Hanc	784.47	**Depreciation:**	
Shipping Supp on Hand	98.31	Truck	7,100.00
Postage on Hand	56.93	Office Equip	5,381.00
Expired Insurance		**Accrued Liabilities**	
Office Insurance	$1,564.00	Interest Ex	228.16
Truck Insurance	921.50	Wage Ex	924.36

Student Name_____

HART & SONS
16.4   GENERAL JOURNAL   Page_____

	DATE		DESCRIPTION	PR	DEBIT	CREDIT
1						
2						
3						
4						
5						
6						
7						
8						
9						
10						
11						
12						
13						
14						
15						
16						
17						
18						
19						
20						
21						
22						
23						
24						
25						
26						
27						
28						
29						
30						
31						
32						

16.4 Hart and Sons Adjusting/Closing/Reversing Entries page 2

Student Name_____

HART & SONS
GENERAL JOURNAL

16.4

Page_____

	DATE		DESCRIPTION	PR	DEBIT	CREDIT
1						
2						
3						
4						
5						
6						
7						
8						
9						
10						
11						
12						
13						
14						
15						
16						
17						
18						
19						
20						
21						
22						
23						
24						
25						
26						
27						
28						
29						
30						
31						
32						

Student Name_____

16.4 12.4 & 13.4

GENERAL LEDGER

Account **CASH**   No. 110

	DATE	ITEM	PR	Debit	Credit	BALANCE Debit	BALANCE Credit
Dec	31	Balance				21,839.40	

Account **CASH - PAYROLL**   No. 115

	DATE	ITEM	PR	Debit	Credit	BALANCE Debit	BALANCE Credit
Dec	31	Balance				0	

Account **ACCOUNTS RECEIVABLE**   No. 120

	DATE	ITEM	PR	Debit	Credit	BALANCE Debit	BALANCE Credit
Dec	31	Balance				8797.68	

Account **ALLOWANCE FOR DOUBTFUL ACCOUNTS**   No. 125

	DATE	ITEM	PR	Debit	Credit	BALANCE Debit	BALANCE Credit
Dec	31						139.24

Account **OFFICE SUPPLIES**   No. 130

	DATE	ITEM	PR	Debit	Credit	BALANCE Debit	BALANCE Credit
Dec	31	Balance				710.82	

16.4 (12.4 & 13.4) Hart and Sons General Ledger page 2

Account **OFFICE EQUIPMENT** No. 140

DATE		ITEM	PR	Debit	Credit	BALANCE Debit	BALANCE Credit
Dec	31	Balance				13,541.21	

Account **ALLOWANCE DEPRECIATION OFFICE EQUIPMENT** No. 140

DATE		ITEM	PR	Debit	Credit	BALANCE Debit	BALANCE Credit
Dec	31	Balance					2,683.21

Account **DELIVERY TRUCK** No. 150

DATE		ITEM	PR	Debit	Credit	BALANCE Debit	BALANCE Credit
Dec	31	Balance				27,000.00	

Account **ALLOWANCE FOR DEPRECIATION TRUCK** No. 155

DATE		ITEM	PR	Debit	Credit	BALANCE Debit	BALANCE Credit

Account **INVENTORY** No. 160

DATE		ITEM	PR	Debit	Credit	BALANCE Debit	BALANCE Credit
Dec	31	Balance				8,000.00	

Account **FEDERAL INCOME TAX PAYABLE** No. 205

DATE		ITEM	PR	Debit	Credit	BALANCE Debit	BALANCE Credit
Dec	31	Balance					98.50

Account **FICA PAYABLE** No. 207

DATE		ITEM	PR	Debit	Credit	BALANCE Debit	BALANCE Credit
Dec	31	Balance					229.66

Account **MEDICARE PAYABLE** No. 208

DATE		ITEM	PR	Debit	Credit	BALANCE Debit	BALANCE Credit
Dec	31	Balance					24.36

Account **ACCOUNTS PAYABLE** No. 210

DATE		ITEM	PR	Debit	Credit	BALANCE Debit	BALANCE Credit
Dec	31	Balance					6,113.80

Account **FUTA PAYABLE** No. 220

DATE		ITEM	PR	Debit	Credit	BALANCE Debit	BALANCE Credit
Dec	31	Balance					107.44

Account **STATE EMPLOYMENT PAYABLE** No. 222

DATE		ITEM	PR	Debit	Credit	BALANCE Debit	BALANCE Credit
Dec	31	Balance					67.15

Account **INTEREST PAYABLE** No. 225

DATE		ITEM	PR	Debit	Credit	BALANCE Debit	BALANCE Credit

Account **WAGES PAYABLE**   No. 230

DATE	ITEM	PR	Debit	Credit	BALANCE Debit	Credit

Account **NOTES PAYABLE**   No. 240

DATE	ITEM	PR	Debit	Credit	BALANCE Debit	Credit
Dec 31	Balance					19,500.00

Account **HART & SONS, CAPITAL**   No. 310

DATE	ITEM	PR	Debit	Credit	BALANCE Debit	Credit
Dec 31	Balance					41,930.72

Account **HART & SONS, DRAWING**   No. 315

DATE	ITEM	PR	Debit	Credit	BALANCE Debit	Credit
Dec 31	Balance				500.00	

Account **INCOME SUMMARY**   No. 330

DATE	ITEM	PR	Debit	Credit	BALANCE Debit	Credit

Account **SALES**   No. 410

DATE	ITEM	PR	Debit	Credit	BALANCE Debit	BALANCE Credit
Dec 31	Balance					38,209.59

Account **SALES DISCOUNT**   No. 415

DATE	ITEM	PR	Debit	Credit	BALANCE Debit	BALANCE Credit
Dec 31	Balance				480.99	

Account **SALES RETURNS AND ALLOWANCES**   No. 420

DATE	ITEM	PR	Debit	Credit	BALANCE Debit	BALANCE Credit
Dec 31	Balance				939.00	

Account **PURCHASES**   No. 510

DATE	ITEM	PR	Debit	Credit	BALANCE Debit	BALANCE Credit
Dec 31	Balance				23,736.60	

Account **PURCHASES DISCOUNT**   No. 515

DATE	ITEM	PR	Debit	Credit	BALANCE Debit	BALANCE Credit
Dec 31	Balance					347.44

16.4 (12.4 & 13.4) Hart and Sons General Ledger page 6

Account **PURCHASES RETURNS AND ALLOWANCES**   No. 520

DATE		ITEM	PR	Debit	Credit	BALANCE Debit	BALANCE Credit
Dec	31	Balance					693.00

Account **RENT EXPENSE**   No. 525

DATE		ITEM	PR	Debit	Credit	BALANCE Debit	BALANCE Credit
Dec	31	Balance				2,400.00	

Account **EMPLOYER PAYROLL EXPENSES**   No. 530

DATE		ITEM	PR	Debit	Credit	BALANCE Debit	BALANCE Credit
Dec	31	Balance				301.60	

Account **DOUBTFUL ACCOUNTS EXPENSE**   No. 535

DATE		ITEM	PR	Debit	Credit	BALANCE Debit	BALANCE Credit
						740.53	

Account **UTILITIES EXPENSE**   No. 540

DATE		ITEM	PR	Debit	Credit	BALANCE Debit	BALANCE Credit
Dec	31	Balance				520.00	

Account **WAGE EXPENSE**   No. 545

						BALANCE	
DATE		ITEM	PR	Debit	Credit	Debit	Credit
Dec	30	Balance				1,343.00	

Account **DEPRECIATION EXPENSE**   No. 555

						BALANCE	
DATE		ITEM	PR	Debit	Credit	Debit	Credit

Account **OFFICE SUPPLIES EXPENSE**   No. 560

						BALANCE	
DATE		ITEM	PR	Debit	Credit	Debit	Credit
Dec	30	Balance				28.98	

Account **INTEREST EXPENSE**   No. 565

						BALANCE	
DATE		ITEM	PR	Debit	Credit	Debit	Credit

Account **MISCELLANEOUS EXPENSE**   No. 575

						BALANCE	
DATE		ITEM	PR	Debit	Credit	Debit	Credit
Dec	31	Balance				4.83	

Student Name_____

HART & SON
Post Closing Trial Balance

16.4   Page_____

	ACCOUNT NAME		
1			
2			
3			
4			
5			
6			
7			
8			
9			
10			
11			
12			
13			
14			
15			
16			
17			
18			
19			
20			
21			
22			
23			
24			
25			
26			
27			
28			
29			
30			
31			

Student Name_____

MEG'S MUFFLER SHOP
17.1 GENERAL JOURNAL

Page_____

	DATE		DESCRIPTION	PR	DEBIT	CREDIT
1						
2						
3						
4						
5						
6						
7						
8						
9						
10						
11						
12						
13						
14						
15						
16						

1						
2						
3						
4						
5						
6						
7						
8						
9						
10						
11						

17.2 Marquita's Boutique

Student Name_____

Marquita's Boutique

17.2 **CASH JOURNAL** Page_____

CASH		DATE		DESCRIPTION	Post	GENERAL	
Debit	Credit	Month	Day		Ref	Debit	Credit

17.3 Student Name_____

MOLLY ELOISE MATERIALS
Income Statement

	Account													
1														
2														
3														
4														
5														
6														
7														
8														
9														
10														
11														
12														
13														
14														
15														
16														
17														
18														
19														
20														
21														
22														
23														
24														
25														
26														
27														
28														
29														
30														
32														

Student Name_____

17.3

MOLLY ELOISE MATERIALS
Capital Statement

	Account													
1														
2														
3														
4														
5														
6														

MOLLY ELOISE MATERIALS
Balance Sheet

	Account													
1														
2														
3														
4														
5														
6														
7														
8														
9														
10														
11														
12														
13														
14														
15														
16														
17														
18														
19														
20														
21														
22														
23														
24														
25														
26														
27														
28														
29														
30														

Student Name_____

Mallett and Foote

18.1   # GENERAL JOURNAL   Page_____

	DATE		DESCRIPTION	PR		DEBIT		CREDIT
1								
2								
3								
4								
5								
6								
7								
8								
9								
10								
11								

CAPITAL STATEMENT
Mallett and Foote Partnership
December 31, 2012

1								
2								
3								
4								
5								
6								
7								
8								
9								
10								
11								
12								
13								
14								
15								
16								

Student Name_____

We Care Lawn Care
18.2   **GENERAL JOURNAL**   Page_____

	DATE		DESCRIPTION	PR	DEBIT	CREDIT
1						
2						
3						
4						
5						
6						
7						
8						
9						
10						
11						
12						
13						
14						
15						
16						
17						
18						
19						
20						
21						
22						
23						
24						
25						
26						
27						
28						
29						

Student Name_____

Molly Eloise Materials
18.3   **GENERAL JOURNAL**   Page_____

	DATE		DESCRIPTION	PR	DEBIT	CREDIT
1						
2						
3						
4						
5						
6						
7						
8						
9						
10						
11						
12						
13						
14						
15						
16						
17						
18						
19						
20						
21						
22						
23						
24						
25						
26						
27						
28						
29						
30						
31						
32						

Student Name_____

Molly Eloise Materials
18.3 GENERAL JOURNAL   Page_____

	DATE		DESCRIPTION	PR	DEBIT	CREDIT
1						
2						
3						
4						
5						
6						
7						
8						
9						
10						
11						
12						
13						
14						
15						
16						
17						
18						
19						
20						
21						
22						
23						
24						
25						
26						
27						
28						
29						
30						
31						
32						